A ROOKIE READER®

TRUCK STOP

By Bonnie Dobkin

Illustrated by Tom Dunnington

Prepared under the direction of Robert Hillerich, Ph.D.

 CHILDRENS PRESS®

CHICAGO

For Adam and Stacey

Library of Congress Cataloging-in-Publication Data

Dobkin, Bonnie
    Truck stop / by Bonnie Dobkin; illustrated by Tom
Dunnington.
        p.   cm. — (A Rookie reader)
    Summary: Describes in verse different kinds of
trucks.
    ISBN 0-516-02027-7
    [1. Trucks—Fiction. 2. Stories in rhyme.]
    I. Dunnington, Tom, ill. II. Title. III. Series.
PZ8.3.D634Tr   1994
[E]—dc20   94-20847
                                                     CIP
                                                      AC

Rushing down the highway,
rolling down the road.

Truck Stop.

Stop, truck!

Come and rest your load.

3

Pick-up truck heads off to work

filled with tools and bags of dirt.

What are dump trucks all about?

First they fill up, then spill out!

7

Big cement trucks can't be beat

when it's time to build a street.

Moving van is packed today.
Someone's moving far away.

13

How do horses go for rides?

This truck carries them inside!

HILL

ORSE FARM

GI3I7

What's inside this tanker truck?
Milk from dairies fills it up.

Meat and eggs and fruit for meals

come in this icebox on wheels!

Tow trucks are a welcome sight

when a car breaks down at night.

Gifts for Josh or Meg or Dan
come in this delivery van.

Everything we throw away

garbage trucks clean up each day.

29

Rushing down the highway,
rolling down the road.
Truck Stop.
Stop, truck!
Come and rest your load.

WORD LIST

			street
a	down	it's	tanker
about	dump	Josh	the
all	each	load	them
and	eggs	meals	then
are	everything	meat	they
at	far	Meg	this
away	fill	milk	throw
bags	filled	moving	time
be	fills	night	to
beat	first	of	today
big	for	off	tools
breaks	from	on	tow
build	fruit	or	truck
can't	garbage	out	trucks
car	gifts	packed	up
carries	go	pick-up	van
cement	heads	rest	we
clean	highway	rides	welcome
come	horses	road	what
dairies	how	rolling	what's
Dan	icebox	rushing	wheels
day	in	sight	when
delivery	inside	someone's	with
dirt	is	spill	work
do	it	stop	your

About the Author

Bonnie Dobkin grew up with the last name Bierman in Morton Grove, Illinois. She attended Maine East High School and later received a degree in education from the University of Illinois. A high-school teacher for several years, Bonnie eventually moved into educational publishing and now works as an executive editor. She lives in Arlington Heights, Illinois.

For story ideas, Bonnie relies on her three sons, Bryan, Michael, and Kevin; her husband Jeff, a dentist; and Kelsey, a confused dog of extremely mixed heritage. When not writing, Bonnie focuses on her other interests—music, community theatre, and chocolate.

About the Artist

Tom Dunnington divides his time between book illustrations and wildlife painting. He has done many books for Childrens Press, as well as working on textbooks, and is a regular contributor to "Highlights for Children." Tom lives in Oak Park, Illinois.